C000229997

FRIENDSHIP
Growing Side by Side

10 studies
for individuals or groups

Carolyn Nystrom

With Notes for Leaders

Scripture Union is an international Christian charity working with churches in more than 130 countries.

Thank you for purchasing this book. Any profits from this book support SU in England and Wales to bring the good news of Jesus Christ to children, young people and families and to enable them to meet God through the Bible and prayer.

Find out more about our work and how you can get involved at:

www.scriptureunion.org.uk (England and Wales)
www.suscotland.org.uk (Scotland)
www.suni.co.uk (Northern Ireland)
www.scriptureunion.org (USA)
www.su.org.au (Australia)

ISBN 978 1 78506 296 4

First published in the United States by InterVarsity Press.
© Carolyn Nystrom

First published in the United Kingdom © Scripture Union 2001, reprinted 2003, 2009, 2010; this edition 2015, reprinted 2016.

British Library Cataloguing-in-Publication data: a catalogue record for this book is available from the British Library.

Printed in Malta by Gutenberg Press Ltd.

Image credit: RelaxFoto.de/iStock by Getty Images

Contents

Getting the Most Out of
Friendship

I didn't have many friends when I was growing up. There were lots of reasons: I lived in a rural community without transportation; there were economic differences between our family and those around us (I was poor); my church emphasized separation; my family masked its fear of outsiders by intentionally closing itself off; my bookish nature—in a culture that valued action and practicality. (Students with A's were not welcomed in my high school—except by a few teachers who weren't welcomed either.) But lest I attach all blame for my friendlessness to outside influences, I now know that my own arrogance was insufferable to those few who might have been willing to climb the barriers toward friendship.

There were advantages to this early deprivation of friendship. I learned to enjoy solitude. I learned to find personal projects that bring me satisfaction. (I've never been bored for more than an hour or two in my life.) I learned independence. It mystified me in college that other students ran around trying to find someone to go to meals with them; I just went to the dining hall and ate. I also learned to think and act without being overly concerned about what other people thought of me.

But friendless people can become selfish people. If I had remained on the fringes of friendship, I think I might have become a rather rigid, self-pleasing person who rarely entered the painful grit of someone else's life—and experienced little support in my own painful grit. God, in his kindness, did not allow that to happen. College years brought people able to scramble over the barriers; I tasted the comradery of like-minded people and went out looking for more.

One by one God has broken down my barriers with an appropriate friend at just the right spot. Did I think that committed Christians were blind to intellectual rigors? God blessed my life with Mark Noll. Did I think that wealthy people were mercenary? God sent me "Alice." Did I think that serious Christians lacked creativity? God introduced me to Luci Shaw. Did I think that I could receive wise counsel only from those who shared my faith? God sat me down in Barry's office. Did I think I wanted to give but not receive? God introduced me to grief.

God created us as beings who thrive in the presence of each other. The writer of Ecclesiastes tells us in simple terms, "If one falls down, his friend can help him up." (Independence is great, but some of the tumbles we take in life are more than we can survive alone.) Later the passage adds, "How can one keep warm alone?" (A bed warmed by a spouse who is a friend or a warm cup of tea with a sisterly friend provides physical warmth and emotional comfort.) Proverbs adds, "As iron sharpens iron, so one man sharpens another." (Friendship brings abrasion, even real pain. But as we bump against each other in our conflicts, we rub off those edges that keep us from being all God has designed.) And that design doesn't end with this life. The God who knew us when we were still in our mother's womb is creating eternity for us where we will live together with him—as his friends.

The Bible talks about friendship, but it doesn't dwell on the subject. Instead, over and over the Bible shows us examples of friendship in practice. This guide provides an opening study that introduces us to biblical reasons for friendship. Next are four pairs of studies. In each pair, the first study introduces a characteristic of godly friendship; the second lets you look at biblical friends who put that quality to work. Finally, we look at Christ's promised return to earth and our friendship with him that lasts an eternity.

May this work enrich your relationships here and encourage you about the life to come.

Suggestions for Individual Study

1. As you begin each study, pray that God will speak to you through his Word.

2. Read the introduction to the study and respond to the personal reflection question or exercise. This is designed to help you focus on

God and on the theme of the study.

3. Each study deals with a particular passage—so that you can delve into the author's meaning in that context. Read and reread the passage to be studied. The questions are written using the language of the New International Version, so you may wish to use that version of the Bible. The New Revised Standard Version is also recommended.

4. This is an inductive Bible study, designed to help you discover for yourself what Scripture is saying. The study includes three types of questions. *Observation* questions ask about the basic facts: who, what, when, where and how. *Interpretation* questions delve into the meaning of the passage. *Application* questions help you discover the implications of the text for growing in Christ. These three keys unlock the treasures of Scripture.

Write your answers to the questions in the spaces provided or in a personal journal. Writing can bring clarity and deeper understanding of yourself and of God's Word.

5. It might be good to have a Bible dictionary handy. Use it to look up any unfamiliar words, names or places.

6. Use the prayer suggestion to guide you in thanking God for what you have learned and to pray about the applications that have come to mind.

7. You may want to go on to the suggestion under "Now or Later," or you may want to use that idea for your next study.

Suggestions for Members of a Group Study

1. Come to the study prepared. Follow the suggestions for individual study mentioned above. You will find that careful preparation will greatly enrich your time spent in group discussion.

2. Be willing to participate in the discussion. The leader of your group will not be lecturing. Instead, he or she will be encouraging the members of the group to discuss what they have learned. The leader will be asking the questions that are found in this guide.

3. Stick to the topic being discussed. Your answers should be based on the verses which are the focus of the discussion and not on outside authorities such as commentaries or speakers. These studies focus on a particular passage of Scripture. Only rarely should you refer to other portions of the Bible. This allows for everyone to participate in in-depth study on equal ground.

4. Be sensitive to the other members of the group. Listen attentively when they describe what they have learned. You may be surprised by their insights! Each question assumes a variety of answers. Many questions do not have "right" answers, particularly questions that aim at meaning or application. Instead the questions push us to explore the passage more thoroughly.

When possible, link what you say to the comments of others. Also, be affirming whenever you can. This will encourage some of the more hesitant members of the group to participate.

5. Be careful not to dominate the discussion. We are sometimes so eager to express our thoughts that we leave too little opportunity for others to respond. By all means participate! But allow others to also.

6. Expect God to teach you through the passage being discussed and through the other members of the group. Pray that you will have an enjoyable and profitable time together, but also that as a result of the study you will find ways that you can take action individually and/or as a group.

7. Remember that anything said in the group is considered confidential and should not be discussed outside the group unless specific permission is given to do so.

8. If you are the group leader, you will find additional suggestions at the back of the guide.

1

Needing Friends

People vary in their friendship patterns. Some have long-term friendships, relationships they have cherished from childhood. Others enjoy the challenge of frequent moves and shaping new friendships in each new home. Some people want a host of casual friends, a roomful of noise and laughter. Others choose only a few friends, preferring long talks and comfortable silence. But people without friends can usually be described with one word: lonely.

GROUP DISCUSSION. What is one of your favorite stories or memories about you and a friend?

PERSONAL REFLECTION. How satisfied are you with your current patterns of friendship? What areas do you think most need attention?

An ancient wisdom writer, who was questioning whether anything could bring meaning to life, discovered that friends were among the few worthwhile pursuits. *Read Ecclesiastes 4:1-12.*

1. What phrases here help you see the writer's view of the world?

2. What specific complaints does the writer have about society (v. 1)?

about work (vv. 4-6)?

3. Note the number of times the writer says that life is meaningless. Why does he say this?

4. What statements in verses 1-6 do you agree with? Why?

5. If you were a friend to the writer of this text, what would you say to him?

6. Finally, in verses 9-12, the author poses one solution to his despair: a friend. What practical value does he see in friendship?

7. What are some ways that these small practical helps from a friend might dent the despair the writer expressed in verses 1-3?

8. Christian couples often choose the words of verse 12 as a wedding theme: "A cord of three strands is not quickly broken." If two friends (or marriage partners) invite God as the third strand in their cord of friendship, what impact would that have on their relationship?

What impact would a three-stranded cord that included God have on the complaints raised in the earlier section of the chapter?

9. Many people today live with the same despair expressed in Ecclesiastes 4:2-3. Who among your acquaintances needs your friendship? What steps could you make in that direction?

Friends are a gift from God. As you pray, mention several of your friends by name, and tell God what you appreciate about each person.

Now or Later

The book of Proverbs offers short wise sayings on many subjects—including friendship. *Read Proverbs 27:6, 10 and 17.* What do you find to be wise in these words?

When and how have you experienced one of these sayings to be true?

2

David &
Mephibosheth

We all *need* friends, but some friends come with their own set of needs—some of those needs with risks attached. King David lived in an era when kings killed their competitors. He'd spent a decade or more on the receiving end of that threat. Saul, the first king of Israel, wanted David dead. David had dodged spears, hidden in caves, even endured Saul's efforts to recruit his wife as a spy. But friendship softened (and complicated) this battle between king and future king. David had sworn eternal friendship to Saul's son Jonathan. Yet Jonathan's children would be Saul's grandchildren as well—potential heirs to the throne. Political savvy said, "Forget the friendship; wipe them out!"

GROUP DISCUSSION. If you were experiencing a time of physical or emotional need, what kind of help would you want from a friend? What would you not want?

PERSONAL REFLECTION. Reflect on one of your long-term friendships. When have you had an opportunity to serve your friend in a time of need? (Or, when and how has your friend served you?) How did those times of need impact the future shape of your friendship?

The kingdom of Israel had moved into a new era. Saul was dead and so was Jonathan. David reigned as king. How was David to keep his vow of friendship to Jonathan? *Read 2 Samuel 9.*

1. In what practical ways did David show kindness to Mephibosheth? (Draw information from throughout the passage.)

2. Mephibosheth referred to himself in verse 8 as a "dead dog." What can you imagine would be difficult about his situation in that era?

3. What did David do that allowed Mephibosheth to maintain a sense of dignity in spite of his needs? (Find all that you can.)

4. If you were not able to walk, what kinds of help would you want and not want?

5. What did David risk by taking Mephibosheth and Ziba into his household?

6. Later David's kingdom suffered an internal rebellion—led by his own son Absalom. King David had to run from Jerusalem to keep from being killed. Just as he left, he met Ziba. *Read 2 Samuel 16:1-4.* How did Ziba return David's favors?

7. How did Ziba explain his presence and Mephibosheth's absence?

8. The rebellion ended. Absalom died. David returned, still in power, to the capital city. *Read 2 Samuel 19:24-30.* How did Mephibosheth's story differ from what Ziba had said?

9. Which story do you think David believed? Explain. (Compare 16:4 with 19:29.)

10. Being a friend to a person in need always involves inconvenience and sometimes real risk. What all might David have lost because of his friendship with Mephibosheth?

11. What inconveniences or risks would come with being a friend to some of the needy people you know?

Despite these obstacles, what sort of commitment do you think God might be calling you to?

Make a quick list of some of the needy people you know. These might be people with physical, emotional or financial needs, or even people who have special needs because of their life stages—a young mother, an aging relative, a person who has recently experienced grief or divorce. One by one, name these people before God in prayer.

Now or Later

Select one person from the list of needy people you prayed for above, a person you are willing to offer your friendship. As you consider what this could cost you (time, money, personal risk), what one or two steps can you take to be a friend to this person? If you need help, select two or three friends to join you in the project. Pray regularly for the person you are serving. Keep journal notes of the events. Look for ways that God is at work. Note any changes you see in yourself.

3

Enjoying Our Differences

City of Refuge in Houston is a church with a difference—lots of them. Its founders planted their church between two neighborhoods: one a mostly black slum, the other a mostly white medical community. The church meets in a homeless shelter straddling the two communities. Staff, elders, teachers, members all reflect that balance. So do the many ministries offered by this church. But no one would say it is easy. There is something about our nature that wants to cozy up to people pretty much like ourselves.

GROUP DISCUSSION. If you were choosing a church (or cluster of friends), what similarities to yourself would help you feel comfortable?

PERSONAL REFLECTION. What differences from yourself would you accept—or even want? Why?

Paul opens this section of his first letter to the Corinthians by saying, "The body is a unit." *Read 1 Corinthians 12:12-31.*

1. Verses 12-19 speak of both unity and diversity. What all unites?

2. Who among your circle of friends represents diversity: a foot, a hand, an eye, an ear?

What do you appreciate about each of these people?

3. Sometimes when we focus on ways we are different from other people, our gut feeling is, "I do not belong" (v. 15). When and why have you felt this way?

4. If your friends accepted the teachings of verses 12-19, what could (or do) they do to help you cope with the feeling of not belonging?

5. Focus on verses 21-26. How would you express what Paul is teaching here?

6. What situations tempt you to think of someone else, "I don't need you" (v. 21)? (Consider your church or fellowship, business, friends, family.)

7. Focus on verses 22-23. How does Paul tell the Corinthians to deal with people who are "weaker," "less honorable," "unpresentable"?

8. What reasons can you find in verses 24-26 for relating to difficult people in this way?

9. Verse 26 speaks of suffering and honor. When has someone chosen to share your suffering—or when has someone allowed you to share his or her honor?

10. Verses 27-31 speak of how individual differences actually strengthen the church. Describe what you would expect to see in a church where these and other skills were seen as gifts from God to be used for the common good.

11. Look at 1 Corinthians 13:1. Why do you think Paul ends this section about diversity among believers with this question?

12. What do you appreciate about this passage that could help you become a better church member, a better worker, a better family member or a better friend?

Quietly read 1 Corinthians 13:1. Focus on your relationships with Christians who shape your own local "body" of believers. Sit in silence, allowing God to bring to your attention ways that you have given and received love within that body. Expect also that he will reveal relationships in which you need to think, speak and behave in a more loving way. Pray about what God reveals to you through this spiritual exercise.

Now or Later

Write a letter (or make a phone call) to a friend. Express appreciation for a particular strength that is different from your own.

4

Naomi & Ruth

Ruth 1—2

Family as friends? Major contrasts lived out in close quarters can make "enjoying our differences" a bitter joke. Creating a sense of family is hard. Maintaining it is even harder. Yet many family members, with God's help, overcome incredible odds and, somewhere in adulthood, become friends. Take, for example, two women from the ancient past: Ruth and her mother-in-law, Naomi.

GROUP DISCUSSION. Describe one family relationship that you have enjoyed.

PERSONAL REFLECTION. If you were to create a visual design of your family's relationships, where would you place yourself: hub? off to the side? linked strongly to some (who?) but not others? (why?). If you were to live by the previous study of enjoying our differences, how might that impact your place in this family design?

Differences within a family make a rocky road toward friendship, but some have walked it well. *Read Ruth 1—2.*

1. What scenes from this story stand out in your mind?

2. What hardships did Ruth and Naomi have to overcome in order to move from a family relationship to a friendship?

3. Study each person's statements about God in the story. How did faith impact the actions of each character?

4. What all did Ruth do to act out the pledge that she made to Naomi in 1:16-17?

5. At the close of the story, Naomi's friends described Ruth as "your daughter-in-law who loves you and who is better to you than seven sons" (4:15). Whose friendship has blessed your life in similar ways? How?

6. In what ways did Boaz show himself as a friend to both Ruth and Naomi in chapter 2?

7. In-law relationships are difficult because they combine families with different values, interests and histories. (Ruth was from the country of Moab, ancient enemies of Naomi's people.) How might family differences also enrich potential friendship? (Give some examples.)

8. What's hard about being an in-law? (Consider the roles of parent-in-law, son- or daughter-in-law, brother- or sister-in-law.)

9. What do you think it would take to be an in-law who is also a friend?

10. Make a list of all your family members. (Include some relatives outside of your immediate family.) Who on this list have you learned to appreciate—in spite of their differences from you? Explain.

11. Which family relationship could be softened by steps toward friendship?

How could you begin those steps?

Gather photos of your family. One by one, cup a photo of each family member in your hand and pray for that person. Thank God for each. Allow God to draw your attention to particular needs.

Now or Later

Read Ruth 3—4. Notice the negotiations Boaz made with the men at the town gate (4:1-12). What all did he (and they) do to ensure that friendship among them would continue?

As they moved toward creating a new family, the characters in the book of Ruth lived out their faith in God in practical, everyday ways. How could you act on your faith in a way that would make you a better present or future family member?

5

Forgiving Friends

Matthew 18:12-35

It was in *Love Story,* a sappy movie of the 1970s, that we first heard the now-famous line, "Love means never having to say you're sorry." It made some sort of sense in the context. The heroine died a sighing death a few perfect weeks into the relationship. Had she lived longer, the writers would have had to create a different line. Friends can't stay friends without forgiveness.

GROUP DISCUSSION. Say one sentence about yourself using the word *forgive.*

PERSONAL REFLECTION. When has forgiveness (or lack of it) affected one of your friendships? Talk to God about what this reveals about you.

When Jesus taught his followers about forgiveness, he told stories. He also created a series of steps that makes forgiveness possible. *Read Matthew 18:12-20.*

1. Jesus tells of two different situations in these verses. What is your emotional response to each? Explain.

2. What similarities can you find between the parable of the sheep and Christ's instructions about a brother who sins?

3. Study the four opportunities for reconciliation presented to the person who sins (vv. 15-17). What is difficult about each step?

4. Why is it important to do the first step *before* taking any other action?

5. Notice that the goal of this procedure, according to verse 15, is that you may win the other person over. How might each of these steps help a person not to wander farther from God?

6. In verse 21 Peter follows the teachings about attempting to reconcile with people who wander by asking a logical next question, "How many times shall I forgive my brother?" What is risky about trying to forgive someone who has hurt you?

7. *Read Matthew 18:21-35.* Study the two examples of debt collection described here. Find all the similarities that you can (vv. 23-30).

8. What differences do you see?

9. In the first half of the servant parable, the amount owed is a large sum of money. Ten thousand talents represented the highest Greek number combined with the largest Roman unit of money. What does this suggest about the nature of our sin debt to God and the extent of God's forgiveness?

10. What all do you see in verses 31-35 that show how the master viewed lack of forgiveness in his servants?

11. Bring to mind a person that you have had trouble forgiving. In a brief time of silence, ask God's forgiveness for your own lack of forgiveness.

What is one way that you could demonstrate your desire to forgive this person?

Mentally picture what would be of great spiritual, emotional and vocational value to the person you have considered above. One by one, name these gifts, asking God to bless that person with these spiritual riches. Then ask God's help in creating genuine forgiveness within you.

Now or Later

Take a few moments to meditate on your own sins—past and present. What has God forgiven you? Remember that God is the loving shepherd who went out looking for a single sheep who had wandered away. He is the master who forgave his servant all that he owed. Bring your sins to him and ask his forgiveness. Read aloud God's assurance to you as found in Psalm 103:8-13.

6

A Father & His Son

"You're not my friend!" shouted five-year-old David, irate at some small prohibition. "That's right," a firm voice shot back. "I'm not your friend. I'm your mother." A few moments later David was once again cooperation and smiles. A wise mom had established appropriate status differences for this stage, making eventual adult friendship more likely.

GROUP DISCUSSION. Recall a time during your growing-up years when you had a fight or serious disagreement with a brother, sister or other family member. What did you fight about and why? What did this event reveal about each of you?

PERSONAL REFLECTION. What is one of your family relationships in which you have trouble forgiving yourself? Bring this person and your relationship with him or her to God in prayer.

In this Bible-era story, we meet a self-serving five-year-old who had grown to adulthood, still thinking mostly of self. If his family had any hope of continuing as a unit, someone would need to let go. And someone would need undeserved forgiveness. *Read Luke 15:11-32.*

1. Who in this story is most like you? Explain.

_____

2. From the beginning, tell this story in your own words—as if you were the youngest son.

_____

3. What do you think the older son would say about his brother's version of the story?

_____

4. Family forgiveness plays a major part in this story. Focus on each member of the family one at a time. What did each have to forgive in the other two family members?

_____

5. What all did the father do to help the brothers forgive each other?

6. In what ways does the father in this story remind you of God?

7. Glance through this story one more time. If you were to write a continuation that begins five years later, what would you write?

8. If you were the father in this family, what would you want to see five years later?

9. What forgiveness do you hope to see in your own family in the next five years?

10. What one or two steps could you take that might lead toward that forgiveness?

11. Forgiveness can sometimes lead to friendship but not always. Do you think that it is possible for parents and their children ever to become real friends? Explain your response.

---

12. What do you personally need to forgive a parent, child or sibling for? (Or what does one of them need to forgive you for?)

Pray using the words of Psalm 32. When the words of the psalm touch needs for forgiveness within your family, pause and use your own words as you pray for the people and relationships that come to mind.

Now or Later

Who within your extended family feels most like a friend? Thank God for that relationship. Consider ways you can continue to nurture that relationship toward friendship.

7

Friends Accountable to Friends

Galatians 6:1-10

Western culture is rooted in independence. We like to pay our own bills, find our own way, take charge of our own lives. This even extends to matters of the soul. We tend to see the state of our soul as between us and God—alone. Yet Scripture speaks often of God's people encouraging and admonishing each other. Living out our faith is something we do best together.

GROUP DISCUSSION. If you were making a report on your spiritual progress during the past week, what would you say? (Include at least one positive item and one area where you would like to improve.)

PERSONAL REFLECTION. What do you think might be reassuring about some form of spiritual accountability to a friend? What do you find troubling about that possibility?

Paul's letter to the Galatians is a book about Christian freedom. It has even been called the Christian Magna Carta. Yet it closes with instructions about spiritual responsibility for each other within the family of God. *Read Galatians 6:1-10.*

1. What attitudes are Christians to have when they help each other in these various ways? (Try to find something in almost every verse.)

---

2. If you were to live with a group of Christians who function in the way described here, what responsibilities would you expect to have?

What would you expect others to do for you?

---

3. Verse 1 gives particular responsibilities to "you who are spiritual." What words of caution do you find in the rest of the passage?

---

4. Why do you think we must be careful when we try to help someone else get straightened out?

5. Verse 2 says that we are to carry each other's burdens, yet verse 5 says that we should carry our own loads. Why might a responsible Christian expect to do both of these—depending on the circumstances?

6. What kinds of situations might lead you to ask a Christian friend for spiritual guidance?

7. What would be hard about letting someone check up on your spiritual progress?

8. Focus on verse 6. What give-and-take between believers does this verse suggest?

9. In verses 7-10 Paul speaks several times of sowing and reaping. What personal encouragement do you find here?

10. What are some ways that friends can help each other to continue in faith?

---

11. Consider again your response to question 1. If you were to report on your spiritual progress in the week to come, what would you want a friend to ask you at the end of that time?

If you are meeting with a group, divide into pairs and pray for each other about the spiritual progress you hope to make in the coming week. If you are alone, look at your calendar or date book for the week ahead. Bring each day to God in prayer. Ask that he reveal himself to you as you go about the duties of each day.

Now or Later

Galatians 6:2 says that when we carry each other's burdens we fulfill "the law of Christ." We can't be sure which specific law Paul meant, but several statements from Christ may help us. Read Matthew 5:43-44; 7:12; Mark 12:30-31 and Galatians 5:14. If you wanted to help someone through a time of spiritual difficulties, what help for the coming week do you find in these laws?

8

David & Nathan

2 Samuel 11:1—12:25

"I've met someone else," said the soft voice on the phone. "I've left the house; I thought you'd want to know."

I felt as stunned as if I had been jolted by an electric current. Our families had been friends for a quarter of a century. We'd had babies at the same time, taken vacations together, attended each other's family funerals. He was a leader in his church, the spiritual patriarch of his extended family. Now his marriage was at an end—or seemed to be—and maybe his walk with God as well. What were we to do, if anything?

GROUP DISCUSSION. What kinds of situations have led you to wonder if a friend ought to step in and point out what is wrong?

PERSONAL REFLECTION. When have you been thankful that someone confronted you about a potential spiritual lapse? This may have been in person (one-to-one) or through writing, teaching or preaching.

Confrontation is always difficult and sometimes dangerous—especially if the person confronted is a king. *Read 2 Samuel 11.*

1. What bothers you about David's actions in this story?

2. Why do you think Uriah would not go home (11:7-13)?

3. What do Joab's actions (11:14-21) say about his character?

4. If you had been Bathsheba's friend, what would you worry about?

5. If you had been David's friend, what (if anything) would you say to him?

6. This chapter ends with the terse statement, "But the thing David had done displeased the LORD." *Read 2 Samuel 12:1-25.* What connections do you see between Nathan's parable in 12:1-4 and David's actions in the previous chapter?

7. Study Nathan's description of David's life in 12:7-9. What perspective did Nathan offer that David may not have seen (or wanted to see) until this point?

---

8. Once David recognized his sin (12:13), how did he express his faith?

---

9. How do you think this story would have ended differently if Nathan had refused to confront David with what he had done wrong?

---

10. Accountability among friends will at times lead to confrontation, and friendship may not survive this. What measures can we take in friendship that could make healthy confrontation possible?

---

11. In the closing scene of this story, God sends Nathan back to David one more time, where he names David and Bathsheba's newborn son Jedidiah, meaning "loved by God." What comfort does this scene offer you about your own life and the lives of your friends?

God is a redeeming God. He confronts the sin of his people, brings us out of it and restores us to himself. Reflect on ways and times God has done this in your own life—and thank him.

Now or Later

As you observe God in this story, what warnings or reassurances do you find in regard to your own actions? (Be as specific as you can.)

9

Loving Friends

In *The Four Loves,* C. S. Lewis contrasts friendship love with other forms of love: "Lovers are normally face to face, absorbed in each other," writes Lewis; "friends side by side, absorbed in some common interest." And later, "The typical expression of opening friendship would be something like, 'What? You too? I thought I was the only one.' "

GROUP DISCUSSION. Who was your best friend during your growing-up years? How did you and your friend show that you cared about each other?

PERSONAL REFLECTION. As you consider your ability to give and receive friendship love, what are some of the barriers you cope with? When have you enjoyed (or missed) opportunities for loving friendship?

John's first letter has sometimes been termed a "love letter." But it is not romantic love that John speaks of. It is love between God and his people and between Christians who (because of God's love) can love one another. *Read 1 John 4:7-21.*

1. Six times in this letter (twice in this passage) John uses the phrase "Dear friends." Would you want to be a friend to a person who could write this kind of letter? Why or why not?

2. John uses the word *love* twenty-seven times in this short section of his letter. What all does he teach us here about God's love?

3. Verse 19 says, "We love because he first loved us." According to this passage, what impact should God's love have on our own attempts to love? (Find all that you can.)

4. What would you expect to see in a person who tries to imitate the love of God as it is described here?

5. Why do you think John draws such a strong link between loving God and loving each other?

6. Verse 10 describes God's love as an "atoning sacrifice." What sacrifices have various people made in their love for you?

7. What kinds of sacrifices has your love for someone else required?

8. Verse 16 says, "God is love." How is that different from saying, "Love is God"?

9. Verse 18 says, "There is no fear in love. But perfect love drives out fear." Why are love and fear sometimes mixed in our human forms of love?

10. As you think through love as it is described in this passage, what are you particularly thankful for?

11. When has a friend offered you some aspect of love as it is described in this passage?

12. What current relationship would you like to enrich by bringing some of the ingredients of love described here?

How can you begin that process?

Review Christ's great commands to "love the Lord your God with all your heart and with all your soul and with all your strength and with all your mind" and "love your neighbor as yourself" (Luke 10:27). Thank God for ways you have been able to give and receive love between friends. In prayer, confess any of your shortcomings that this standard of love brings to mind.

Now or Later

Read 1 John 3:1-10. Picture yourself as a child of God hearing these words of love for you. Thank him for what he offers you in these verses. Offer your own love in return.

10

Forever Friends

Long-term friendships are special. Together we remember major life events: kindergarten, graduation, weddings, births. We've shared minutia: a favorite flavor of tea, a silly joke—or fear. We have disagreed, gotten angry and gotten over it. But Christian friendship brings new meaning to *long-term*.

GROUP DISCUSSION. Describe one of your long-standing friendships. (Who is it with? How did you meet? Why and how did you remain friends?)

PERSONAL REFLECTION. What is one of your favorite mental images of heaven? Who are you with? What are you doing? What changes do you see in yourself?

The Christians of Thessalonica had a question. They knew that Christ would return; he had told them so. But what about Christians who had already died? Would they miss his return? Does death separate Christians forever, or . . . ? *Read 1 Thessalonians 4:13-18.*

1. What visual images does this passage present?

2. Paul begins this passage by saying that Christians do not grieve like people who have no hope (4:13). What part does Christ play in the hope offered here?

3. Paul ends this section by saying, "Therefore encourage each other with these words" (4:18). What do you find encouraging in these verses?

4. Try to picture yourself with a dear friend (even one who has died), alive together in the scene described here. What images and feelings come to your mind?

5. *Read 1 Thessalonians 5:1-11.* What words and phrases suggest warning?

6. Paul speaks here of two kinds of people, those who belong to darkness and those who belong to light. How, according to the text, are these people different from each other?

7. In 5:8 Paul says that one of the protections against the warnings described here is "the hope of salvation." What is salvation (5:9-10)?

Why is it a hope?

_____

8. In view of the warnings and the promise here, what would you encourage a friend to do or to be?

_____

9. First Thessalonians 4:17 tells us that we will be "with the Lord forever," and 5:10 adds that we will "live together with him." If some of your friendships are in fact eternal relationships, how might that affect the way you conduct them now?

Use this passage as an outline for prayer. Thank God for what he offers you throughout these verses.

Now or Later

During your ten studies on friendship, you have thought of many of your friends—past and present. Bring these friends to mind, one by one. Are there any who need the encouragement, comfort or warning that comes from this passage? Consider how you might live out this passage in actions or conversation as you continue these friendships.

Leader's Notes

MY GRACE IS SUFFICIENT FOR YOU. (2 COR 12:9)

Leading a Bible discussion can be an enjoyable and rewarding experience. But it can also be *scary*—especially if you've never done it before. If this is your feeling, you're in good company. When God asked Moses to lead the Israelites out of Egypt, he replied, "O Lord, please send someone else to do it!" (Ex 4:13). It was the same with Solomon, Jeremiah and Timothy, but God helped these people in spite of their weaknesses, and he will help you as well.

You don't need to be an expert on the Bible or a trained teacher to lead a Bible discussion. The idea behind these inductive studies is that the leader guides group members to discover for themselves what the Bible has to say. This method of learning will allow group members to remember much more of what is said than a lecture would.

These studies are designed to be led easily. As a matter of fact, the flow of questions through the passage from observation to interpretation to application is so natural that you may feel that the studies lead themselves. This study guide is also flexible. You can use it with a variety of groups— student, professional, neighborhood or church groups. Each study takes forty-five to sixty minutes in a group setting.

There are some important facts to know about group dynamics and encouraging discussion. The suggestions listed below should enable you to effectively and enjoyably fulfill your role as leader.

Preparing for the Study

1. Ask God to help you understand and apply the passage in your own life. Unless this happens, you will not be prepared to lead others. Pray too for the various members of the group. Ask God to open your hearts to the message of his Word and motivate you to action.

2. Read the introduction to the entire guide to get an overview of the entire book and the issues which will be explored.

3. As you begin each study, read and reread the assigned Bible passage to familiarize yourself with it.

4. This study guide is based on the New International Version of the Bible. It will help you and the group if you use this translation as the basis for your study and discussion.

5. Carefully work through each question in the study. Spend time in meditation and reflection as you consider how to respond.

6. Write your thoughts and responses in the space provided in the study guide. This will help you to express your understanding of the passage clearly.

7. It might help to have a Bible dictionary handy. Use it to look up any unfamiliar words, names or places. (For additional help on how to study a passage, see chapter five of *How to Lead a LifeGuide Bible Study,* InterVarsity Press.)

8. Consider how you can apply the Scripture to your life. Remember that the group will follow your lead in responding to the studies. They will not go any deeper than you do.

9. Once you have finished your own study of the passage, familiarize yourself with the leader's notes for the study you are leading. These are designed to help you in several ways. First, they tell you the purpose the study guide author had in mind when writing the study. Take time to think through how the study questions work together to accomplish that purpose. Second, the notes provide you with additional background information or suggestions on group dynamics for various questions. This information can be useful when people have difficulty understanding or answering a question. Third, the leader's notes can alert you to potential problems you may encounter during the study.

10. If you wish to remind yourself of anything mentioned in the leader's notes, make a note to yourself below that question in the study.

Leading the Study
1. Begin the study on time. Open with prayer, asking God to help the group to understand and apply the passage.

2. Be sure that everyone in your group has a study guide. Encourage the group to prepare beforehand for each discussion by reading the introduction to the guide and by working through the questions in the study.

3. At the beginning of your first time together, explain that these studies are meant to be discussions, not lectures. Encourage the members of the group to participate. However, do not put pressure on those who may be hesitant to speak during the first few sessions. You may want to suggest the following guidelines to your group.
☐ Stick to the topic being discussed.

☐ Your responses should be based on the verses which are the focus of the discussion and not on outside authorities such as commentaries or speakers.

☐ These studies focus on a particular passage of Scripture. Only rarely should you refer to other portions of the Bible. This allows for everyone to participate in in-depth study on equal ground.

☐ Anything said in the group is considered confidential and will not be discussed outside the group unless specific permission is given to do so.

☐ We will listen attentively to each other and provide time for each person present to talk.

☐ We will pray for each other.

4. Have a group member read the introduction at the beginning of the discussion.

5. Every session begins with a group discussion question. The question or activity is meant to be used before the passage is read. The question introduces the theme of the study and encourages group members to begin to open up. Encourage as many members as possible to participate, and be ready to get the discussion going with your own response.

This section is designed to reveal where our thoughts or feelings need to be transformed by Scripture. That is why it is especially important not to read the passage before the discussion question is asked. The passage will tend to color the honest reactions people would otherwise give because they are, of course, supposed to think the way the Bible does.

You may want to supplement the group discussion question with an icebreaker to help people to get comfortable. See the community section of *Small Group Idea Book* for more ideas.

You also might want to use the personal reflection question with your group. Either allow a time of silence for people to respond individually or discuss it together.

6. Have a group member (or members if the passage is long) read aloud the passage to be studied. Then give people several minutes to read the passage again silently so that they can take it all in.

7. Question 1 will generally be an overview question designed to briefly survey the passage. Encourage the group to look at the whole passage, but try to avoid getting sidetracked by questions or issues that will be addressed later in the study.

8. As you ask the questions, keep in mind that they are designed to be used just as they are written. You may simply read them aloud. Or you may prefer to express them in your own words.

There may be times when it is appropriate to deviate from the study guide.

For example, a question may have already been answered. If so, move on to the next question. Or someone may raise an important question not covered in the guide. Take time to discuss it, but try to keep the group from going off on tangents.

9. Avoid answering your own questions. If necessary, repeat or rephrase them until they are clearly understood. Or point out something you read in the leader's notes to clarify the context or meaning. An eager group quickly becomes passive and silent if they think the leader will do most of the talking.

10. Don't be afraid of silence. People may need time to think about the question before formulating their answers.

11. Don't be content with just one answer. Ask, "What do the rest of you think?" or "Anything else?" until several people have given answers to the question.

12. Acknowledge all contributions. Try to be affirming whenever possible. Never reject an answer. If it is clearly off-base, ask, "Which verse led you to that conclusion?" or again, "What do the rest of you think?"

13. Don't expect every answer to be addressed to you, even though this will probably happen at first. As group members become more at ease, they will begin to truly interact with each other. This is one sign of healthy discussion.

14. Don't be afraid of controversy. It can be very stimulating. If you don't resolve an issue completely, don't be frustrated. Move on and keep it in mind for later. A subsequent study may solve the problem.

15. Periodically summarize what the group has said about the passage. This helps to draw together the various ideas mentioned and gives continuity to the study. But don't preach.

16. At the end of the Bible discussion you may want to allow group members a time of quiet to work on an idea under "Now or Later." Then discuss what you experienced. Or you may want to encourage group members to work on these ideas between meetings. Give an opportunity during the session for people to talk about what they are learning.

17. Conclude your time together with conversational prayer, adapting the prayer suggestion at the end of the study to your group. Ask for God's help in following through on the commitments you've made.

18. End on time.

Many more suggestions and helps are found in *How to Lead a LifeGuide Bible Study.*

Components of Small Groups
A healthy small group should do more than study the Bible. There are four

components to consider as you structure your time together.

Nurture. Small groups help us to grow in our knowledge and love of God. Bible study is the key to making this happen and is the foundation of your small group.

Community. Small groups are a great place to develop deep friendships with other Christians. Allow time for informal interaction before and after each study. Plan activities and games that will help you get to know each other. Spend time having fun together—going on a picnic or cooking dinner together.

Worship and prayer. Your study will be enhanced by spending time praising God together in prayer or song. Pray for each other's needs—and keep track of how God is answering prayer in your group. Ask God to help you to apply what you are learning in your study.

Outreach. Reaching out to others can be a practical way of applying what you are learning, and it will keep your group from becoming self-focused. Host a series of evangelistic discussions for your friends or neighbors. Clean up the yard of an elderly friend. Serve at a soup kitchen together, or spend a day working on a Habitat house.

Many more suggestions and helps in each of these areas are found in *Small Group Idea Book*. Information on building a small group can be found in *Small Group Leaders' Handbook* and *The Big Book on Small Groups* (both from Inter-Varsity Press). Reading through one of these books would be worth your time.

Study 1. Needing Friends. Ecclesiastes 4:1-12.

Purpose: To appreciate God's gift of friendship with other people and with himself.

Question 1. If you are meeting with a group, use this question to help people gain an overview of this section of the text. They should point out phrases in almost every verse. If your group has trouble responding to such a comprehensive question, try breaking it down. Ask: Do you see the tone of this passage as optimistic, pessimistic or realistic? What words and phrases in the text cause you to think that?

Question 3. Your group should point out that the man was alone, that wealth did not bring contentment—perhaps because he had no one to share it with and seemed unable to experience joy (v. 8).

Question 4. Verses 1-6 express a variety of complaints, observations and even a suggestion or two. Most of us can identify with one or more of the statements. Use this question to help group members understand each other's perspectives.

Question 5. Encourage people to respond to the author of Ecclesiastes as if he were a friend. Many of us have friends with these complaints. Some of the complaints are our own. Some will agree with this "friend." Others will offer compassion and hope. In this way group members can minister indirectly to each other. They will also gain resources to share with similar friends.

Prayer. You can use this prayer exercise in a couple of ways. At the beginning you can suggest that people tell each other what they appreciate about their various friends (including, perhaps, people in the group). But then remind them that friends are, in fact, a gift from God. So close your time together by offering prayers of thanks as suggested in the note.

Now or Later. These sections provide additional material related to each study. You can work them into the midsection of the discussion, add them at the close of the study or suggest them as a personal follow-up to the group meeting.

Study 2. David & Mephibosheth. 2 Samuel 9; 16:1-4; 19:24-30.
Purpose: To realistically assess the risk of becoming a friend to a needy person and then taking that risk.

Personal reflection. No one lives a trouble-free life. In long-term friendships, one or both members will have experienced need. Prayerfully consider ways that you and your friend have served each other during those times. This study transfers the subject of need in the previous study (our own *need* for friends) to a more outward focus: the *needs* that friends bring with them and how good friends deal with those needs and the accompanying risks. David endured great risk because of his commitment to friendship with Jonathan— and therefore with Jonathan's son.

Question 2. For the story of how Mephibosheth became crippled see 2 Samuel 4:1-4.

Question 3. If you need follow-up questions, consider: "Why do you think that David included Ziba in his help to Mephibosheth?"; "Why did he restore Saul's land to Mephibosheth?"; "What did Mephibosheth gain by eating at David's table?" Answers to these questions should show that David provided a means for Mephibosheth to maintain independence, economic security and dignity. By seating him at the king's table, David gave Mephibosheth respect, not to mention an adequate diet. (Eating at David's table also allowed surveillance, not an unwise decision in view of the events that followed.)

Question 4. Dependence and independence are in constant tension for people unable to walk. So is dignity. Use this question to mentally put yourself in a wheelchair. What kinds of help would allow you to keep some sense of independence and dignity?

Question 5. In answering this question, consider the obvious personal and economic risks but also the political risks reflected in the introduction to this study. In addition, David had some of the same reasons to fear helping Mephibosheth that we fear in our own contacts with people who are needy. Notice the last sentence of verse 10. Ziba's household was no small force of able-bodied men. David must have wondered if he could count on their loyalty—and what might happen to him if they turned against him.

Question 9. If you are meeting with a group, let your group discuss reactions to David's decision. Some may think that Mephibosheth, a "Johnny-come-lately," should have lost his share of the inheritance. Others say that Ziba was lying and should have been banished. Still others agree with David. He couldn't know who was telling the truth, so he was right in dividing the property between them.

Question 10. If you have covered potential answers already, just do a quick recap at this stage. David did give up property and food. He may have lost respect among strong loyalists who viewed his kindness to Saul's son as an unnecessary risk. He might have harbored a traitor and a spy at his own table. He could have lost his kingdom and his life. Even without that, he probably lost his ability to trust either Mephibosheth or Ziba. Still he kept them on as friends and tenants.

Question 11. This is not a spot for quick-fix answers. Even though we don't like this quality in ourselves, many of us avoid real contact with needy people because we don't want to take the risks their needs create. So we house ourselves within barriers by where we choose to work, live, even where we go to church, so that we do not have to see people with serious needs. These barriers protect us not only from inconvenience but also from recognizing our own selfishness. Use this question to take an honest look at some potential risks—even if it is as simple as time taken away from work in order to visit an aging uncle on the way home. Weighing the cost of being a friend to someone in need will help us make realistic decisions about what we are willing to offer.

Study 3. Enjoying Our Differences. 1 Corinthians 12:12-31.
Purpose: To respect and draw on the differences that God has created among his people.

Question 2. Help members of your group to first understand what a foot, hand, eye or ear might do, then name people who especially demonstrate those qualities. For example, a "foot" might be one who is quick to jump in and *do* something. An "ear" might be a person who listens with wisdom, compassion and understanding. If some people name others in the group, the question will help you to express appreciation for each other in a way that reflects the teachings of the passage.

Question 7. Your group should discuss the acceptance and protection expressed in the words *indispensable, special honor* and *modesty*. If you have time for a follow-up question at this point, ask: How is Paul's approach toward difficult people different from normal practice?

Question 8. Your group should study such phrases as "God has combined" (v. 24), "so that there should be no division" (v. 25), "equal concern for each other" (v. 25). People should also look at the prospect of suffering and rejoicing together (v. 26).

Question 12. If your group does not move automatically into discussing practical ways to put these observations to work, ask: What is one step you could take toward meeting that challenge?

Study 4. Naomi & Ruth. Ruth 1—2.
Purpose: To allow our faith in God to grow us into people who have the ability to become friends with members of our families.

Question 2. Your group should find a variety of hardships as they survey the story. These include: cultural differences (1:2; 2:10), death (1:3, 5), lack of grandchildren (1:5), poverty (1:6; 2:3), bitterness (1:20), danger (2:9), differing homelands (2:10), rival parents (2:11), shared housing (2:23) and unfamiliar customs (2:2-3).

Question 3. Naomi's references to God occur in 1:20-21 and 2:20. Ruth speaks of God in 1:16-18. Boaz mentions God in 2:4, 12. Later in the story, the town elders call on God in 4:11-12, as do Naomi's friends in 4:14-15. As your group members spot each reference, ask that they link the beliefs (implied or stated) with the actions.

Question 4. Your group should outline Ruth's actions in chapter 2.

Question 6. The following references may help: 2:4, 8-12, 14-16.

Questions 10-11. Allow a few moments for people to pencil a list of family members. Then conduct a discussion of these two questions with all of the sensitivity you can muster. (Family relationships are often tense and painful.) Be aware that not everyone will want to speak and that some family relationships are not within our power to repair.

Study 5. Forgiving Friends. Matthew 18:12-35.
Purpose: To forgive our friends in the same way that Christ has forgiven us.

Question 1. If you are leading a group, encourage brief answers here that reflect an emotional response to each story. Most people will see the parable of the sheep in warm, positive tones and the instructions about church discipline as harsh and punitive. Just accept the initial reactions at this point. As the study progresses, your group may begin to see that these two events are quite similar in purpose.

Question 2. Encourage your group to linger long enough on this question to discover several similarities between the two stories. People should notice that both deal with a wanderer, both have the shepherd/brother going to great effort to bring the wanderer back, both show results of the wanderer's return (or loss) in heaven, both speak of celebration if the lost one returns, and both show the great value God holds for the sheep/person who wanders.

Question 4. This is one of Christ's loving commands. It shows people how to forgive by keeping a problem contained "just between the two of them." It also provides an opportunity for two people to better understand each other without spreading what may be false rumors. Disregarding this first step leads to gossip and creates enlarged hostility. Only if this first, private step is totally unsuccessful are we entitled to bring others into the conflict. Even then it is with the hope that a brotherly/sisterly relationship can continue—through repentance and forgiveness (v. 15).

Question 5. Possible reconciliation is fairly obvious in the first three steps, and your group should discuss ways this might occur during the course of each step. But people may have trouble seeing how treating someone as "a pagan or a tax collector" could lead one to return to faith. Jesus may have used this phrase because it was a common synonym in Jewish culture for excommunication. But we must also consider how Jesus himself treated pagans and tax collectors. He healed them (the daughter of the Canaanite woman in Mt 15:21-28), he ate with them (Zacchaeus in Lk 19:1-10), he even called one to become his disciple (Matthew [Levi] in Mk 2:13-17). So Jesus may have intended that we treat this persistent wanderer with all the kindness (and wariness) that we would treat any outsider we wished to win to faith.

In addition, we must also keep in mind the teachings of Paul in 1 Corinthians 5:1-5, where a person who practiced sexual immorality was to be expelled (temporarily) from the congregation so that "the sinful nature may be destroyed and his spirit saved on the day of the Lord." If you want to analyze this passage further, ask, "How do the words of verses 18-19 give importance to the process described in verses 15-17?" Verse 18 is quite similar to Christ's words to Peter in 16:19. Though we may not know exactly what Jesus meant, we can know that he imparted a strong power to the church to deal with people who might wander from faith. Matthew 18:19-20 is often misused as a recipe for getting what we want from God when we pray. The context, however, assumes a situation of church discipline. It also assumes that prayers "in my name" ask what Jesus himself would give if he were present.

Question 6. This question will begin to lead your group into the area of past hurts and forgiveness. It will help at the outset to talk about the real risks involved. You will be discussing this area at a more personal level before the study is over.

Question 10. Encourage your group to pick out relevant words and phrases from verses 32-35. Obviously God takes unwillingness to forgive quite seriously.

Question 11. If you are leading a group, conduct a time of meditation and prayer following question 11. Then ask who is willing to respond to the second part of the question. Be sensitive to the hurt these questions may reveal. If it seems appropriate, close with a time of prayer for each other that God will heal the pain of these relationships as a first step toward peace and forgiveness.

Study 6. A Father & His Son. Luke 15:11-32.
Purpose: To practice forgiveness as one means of creating friendship with our families.

Group discussion. Encourage a rather lighthearted time of childhood storytelling. The second part of the question may help people gain some perspective on these events, as they helped define and perhaps shape their current character.

Question 1. Characters in the story include the father, the older son, the younger son and the party guests.

Question 2. If you are working with a group, suggest that half of the group listen to the story as if they were the younger son. The other half can listen through the ears of the older son.

Question 4. If your group needs a breakdown of this question, ask: What did the father have to forgive each son (vv. 12-14, 25, 28, 30)? What did each son have to forgive his father? (The younger son probably had to forgive the father for whatever reasons caused him to leave home in the first place. Regarding the older son, see vv. 20, 29, 30.) What did the sons have to forgive each other? (Answers will be similar to those transgressions against the father, except they will appear from the perspective of a brother, who might sustain his own personal losses because of the other's actions.) Encourage your group to work with this question until people are able to see the necessity of each family member giving and receiving forgiveness.

Question 5. Study the father's actions throughout the story, considering how they might lead the sons to forgive each other. Focus especially on the closing conversation presented in verses 28-32.

Question 9. If it seems appropriate for your group, take a few moments at this point for silent or spoken prayers about the family members that they hope will forgive each other.

Question 11. If you want to tackle this subject with smaller questions (and if time permits), ask: What is hard (or impossible) about being a "friend" to your parents? What is hard (or impossible) about being a friend to your child? When did you first begin to think that you might be able to become a friend to one of your parents? to one of your children? What barriers have you seen to friendship between parents and children? How is friendship between a parent and an adult child different from friendship between peers?

Study 7. Friends Accountable to Friends. Galatians 6:1-10.
Purpose: To take responsibility for nurturing spiritual growth in each other.
Group discussion. Try to get two responses from each person. You will use the answers to this question at the close of the session.
Question 1. If you are meeting with a group, help people there to define attitudes reflected by the words *gently* and *humbly* (v. 1). They should also notice the accurate self-evaluation described in verse 3 and the exhortation not to be competitive or put others down in verse 4. Verse 6 shows that we are to be generous, verses 7-8 that we must be aware of consequences, verse 9 that we should be persistent, and verse 10 that we are to be loyal.
Question 2. Your group should draw on information in verses 1-2, 6 and 10.
Question 3. Warnings appear throughout this text. Your group should spot such words and phrases as, "watch yourself" (v. 1), "tempted" (v. 1), "deceive himself" (v. 3), "test his own actions" (v. 4), "God cannot be mocked" (v. 7), "man reaps" (v. 7) and "do not give up" (v. 9).
Question 8. One simple example is that we can expect to give money ("share all good things") to people who give us spiritual instruction. Pastors, seminary teachers and missionaries would fall in this category. But the verse may also suggest that just as the instructors share knowledge and insight with us, we too can share what God has taught us. This reciprocal arrangement is illustrated in the relationship between Paul, Priscilla and Aquila, and Apollos.
Question 11. Encourage as many as are willing to respond. If your group wishes, make a list of intentions for the week and check up on each other's progress at the next meeting time.

58 ———————————————————————— *Friendship*

Study 8. David & Nathan. 2 Samuel 11:1—12:25.
Purpose: To consider why (or whether) we should confront sin in friendships in which we are accountable to each other.

General note. As preparation to lead this session, read passages that deal with the past and future relationship between David and Nathan. These include 2 Samuel 7:1-17; 1 Kings 1:1-14; 4:5; 1 Chronicles 11:38; 29:29-30; 2 Chronicles 29:25-26.

Question 1. If you are meeting with a group, guide people to point out events throughout the chapter. Allow time for comments about personal reactions to what David did. Potential "hot spots" appear in 11:1, 4, 6-8, 14-15, 25 and 27.

Question 2. Opinions may vary. Relevant information appears in verses 7-13. Some in the group may accept Uriah's noble statements in verse 11 at face value. Others may guess that Uriah was aware that something was not right about David's "friendly" gestures.

Question 5. Note David's calloused response in 11:25.

Question 6. If your group needs help with the symbolism here, ask that they figure out who in David's life symbolized the rich man, the poor man and the ewe lamb.

Question 8. Your group should find information in 12:13, 16-17, 20 and 23, as well as the comfort he offered to Bathsheba in 12:24.

Question 11. Help your group to be as personal and specific as possible within the bounds of propriety. This closing scene shows us that not all accountability missions are ugly or confronting. As Nathan brought good news from God, we may also hear and receive commendation from our friends. God gave David a new start. God did not retract his previous promise to David that his descendants would rule Israel. God even passed his love for David on to his new son. Some in your group may notice that if we confess our sins, God may also give us a fresh start—even if we can't fix what we've done wrong. (David could not bring Uriah back to life.) David suffered terrible consequences due to his sin, and more consequences were on the horizon. But God will not hold our shortcomings against us forever. He will keep on loving us. People in your group may thus express hope and comfort in similar situations.

Study 9. Loving Friends. 1 John 4:7-21.
Purpose: To imitate God's love in our relationships with him and with other people.

Group discussion. Use this question to understand each other's history and to appreciate (and even laugh at) childlike ways of expressing friendship love.

Question 1. If you are meeting with a group, this question should help them respond emotionally to John's concept of love while simultaneously conducting a brief survey of the passage.

Question 2. Use this question to help your group examine the text in detail. People should point out information about God's love in almost every verse.

Question 3. This question builds on the previous one—as does the passage itself. Survey the text one more time as you look for links between God's love and our own.

Question 4. Move beyond the text at this point as you encourage your group to speak of practical ways this type of love might show itself in ordinary lives. Be aware that not all outcomes of this type of love will be mutually satisfying. God's love is sacrificial and so, sometimes, is our own.

Questions 6-7. These questions will require more personal answers than the previous ones—and in the difficult area of sacrifice. It is not easy to think of ourselves as being hard to love or as receivers of sacrificial love. Be prepared to offer an example of your own. Most of us will have to admit that we have at some time received sacrificial love from a parent, teacher, friend, spouse or even God. If we are able to admit our own need for receiving sacrificial love, we can become a little less resentful of loving sacrifices we must make toward others.

Question 8. Contemporary society idolizes love. We can do almost anything "for love" and be met with indulgent smiles. This is not the teaching of the passage. Love is part of the core character of God. It describes who he is. But God is also faithful, wise, holy, even wrathful. And love (by itself) is not God. Your group should discuss its way to similar conclusions.

Question 9. The key here is, of course, the word *perfect*. Little in this fallen world is perfect—including love. So we often see fear and love mixed. Your group will think of examples of this mixture. Only God's love is perfect. As we attempt to model God's love (as this passage encourages us to do), we will begin to drive out the fear in our relationships.

Question 10. If you are in a group, encourage each person to respond in some way to this opportunity for personal reflection on the text.

Study 10. Forever Friends. 1 Thessalonians 4:13—5:11.
Purpose: To find comfort, warning and hope in God's offer of eternity together with him.

Question 1. If you are meeting with a group, use this question to help people study the entire passage—especially the vivid images it portrays.

Question 2. Your group should point out Christ's actions throughout this text. Note especially his death and resurrection, as well as the words "and so" in verse 14. Paul's picture of our life after death is rooted in Christ's own victory over death.

Question 3. Survey the passage once again, looking for encouragement. What is encouraging will vary from person to person, but a composite will pick up most of what is in the passage.

Question 5. While the first passage you studied is full of hope and joy, this text mentions several warnings. Your group should mention such phrases as: "thief in the night" (5:2), "destruction" (5:3), "labor pains" (5:3), "not escape" (5:3), "darkness" (5:4), "wrath" (5:9) and others.

Question 6. Your group should study verses 4-9, exploring the variety of contrasts offered here.

Question 7. Verse 7 speaks of salvation as a "helmet," a form of protection. Your group should explain salvation as it is described in this text (vv. 9-10). They will find further explanation in 4:14-18. If some in your group are uncertain about whether they currently belong to the light or the darkness, explain as simply as you can the offer Christ makes. Invite others in your group to do the same.

Prayer. Consider using this as a closing to your group's study of friendship. Invite everyone to pray brief prayers of a sentence or two as they look through the text. For example, you may begin by saying, "Thank you that you give me hope even though I still grieve the death of my mother." Help your group to be comfortable with silence between the prayers by suggesting that God hears our silent prayers as well as our spoken ones.

Carolyn Nystrom is a freelance writer living in St. Charles, Illinois. She has written more than seventy books and Bible study guides.

What Should We Study Next?

A good place to start study of Scripture would be with a book study. Many groups begin with a Gospel, such as *Mark* (20 studies by Jim Hoover) or *John* (26 studies by Douglas Connelly). These guides are divided into two parts, so that if twenty or tweny-six weeks seems like too much to do at once, the group can feel free to do half and take a break with another topic. You might want to come back to it later.

You might prefer to try a smaller letter. *Philippians* (9 studies by Donald Baker), *Ephesians* (13 studies by Andrew T. and Phylis J. Le Peau) and *1 & 2 Timothy and Titus* (12 studies by Pete Sommer) are good options. If you want to vary your reading with an Old Testament book, consider *Ecclesiastes* (12 studies by Bill and Teresa Syrios) for a challenging and exciting study.

There are a number of interesting topical *Lifebuilder* studies as well. Here are some options for filling three or four quarters of a year:

Basic Discpleship
Christian Beliefs – 12 studies by Stephen D. Eyre
Christian Character – 12 studies by Andrea Sterk & Peter Scazzero
Christian Disciplines – 12 studies by Andrea Sterk & Peter Scazzero
Evangelism – 12 studies by Rebecca Pippert & Ruth Siemens

Building Community
Christian Community – 12 studies by Rob Suggs
Fruit of the Spirit – 9 studies by Hazel Offner
Spiritual Gifts – 12 studies by Charles & Anne Hummel

Character Studies
New Testament Characters – 12 studies by Carolyn Nystrom
Old Testament Characters – 12 studies by Peter Scazzero
Old Testament Kings – 12 studies by Carolyn Nystrom
Women of the Old Testament – 12 studies by Gladys Hunt

The Trinity
Meeting God – 12 studies by J. I. Parker
Meeting Jesus – 13 studies by Leighton Ford
Meeting the Spirit – 12 studies by Douglas Connelly

ALSO FOR SMALL GROUPS

As well as over 70 titles in the popular *LifeBuilder* series, Scripture Union produces a wide variety of resources for small groups. Among them are:

WordLive – an innovative online Bible experience for groups and individuals, offering a wide variety of free material: study notes, maps, illustrations, images, poems, meditations, downloadable podcasts, prayer activities. Log on and check it out: www.wordlive.org

The Multi-Sensory series – popular resources for creative small groups, youth groups and churches that appeal to a wide range of learning styles.

Deeper Encounter – for confident groups that have a good understanding of Bible text – containing seven studies, complete with CD audio tracks and photocopiable worksheets.

Top Tips on Leading Small Groups – biblical patterns and practical ideas to inspire leaders of small groups.

Essential 100 and *Essential Jesus* – 100-reading overview of the Bible (*Essential 100*) and the person and work of Jesus (*Essential Jesus*), with notes and helps – presented as a programme for individuals, small groups or whole churches.

Small Groups Growing Churches – a flexible training resource for leading small groups. Can be used as a complete 15-topic training course, for a tailor-made church weekend or for one-off refresher sessions.

SU publications are available from Christian bookshops, on the Internet, or via mail order. Advice on what would suit your group best is always available. You can:

- log on to www.scriptureunion.org.uk
- phone SU's mail order line: 01908 856006
- email info@scriptureunion.org.uk
- fax 01908 856020
- write to SU Mail Order, PO Box 5148, Milton Keynes MLO, MK2 2YX

Scripture Union
Using the Bible to inspire children, young people and adults to know God.

Scripture union

Have you ever asked yourself
How can I make a difference for God?

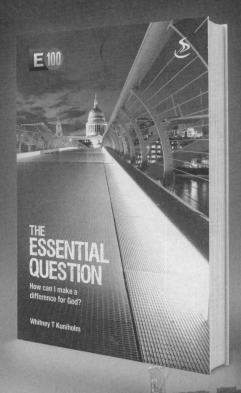

E 100

On some level, we all struggle to find our own answer to that fundamental question. The search for significance is the underlying motivation for virtually all human activity. It's what drives us.

The Essential Question takes you on a journey through the book of Acts. Fifty Bible readings to help you begin to find and follow God's plan for you today.

Single book:
978 1 84427 902 9
£6.99

5-pack also available:
978 1 84427 903 6
£25.00

THE
ESSENTIAL
QUESTION

How can I make a
difference for God?

Whitney T Kuniholm

ESSENTIAL 100

Single book:
978 1 84427 566 3
£6.99

5-pack also available:
978 1 84427 546 5
£25.00

ESSENTIAL JESUS

Single book:
978 184427 238 9
£6.99

5-pack also available:
978 184427 239 6
£25.00

Big Bible Challenge

Single book:
978 1 84427 584 7
£9.99

SCAN HERE
FOR MORE INFO